UNDER THE MICROSCOPE

MINERALS
UP CLOSE

Gareth Stevens
Publishing

BY JASON GLASER

Please visit our website, www.garethstevens.com. For a free color catalog of all our high-quality books, call toll free 1-800-542-2595 or fax 1-877-542-2596.

Library of Congress Cataloging-in-Publication Data

Glaser, Jason.
Minerals up close / Jason Glaser.
     p. cm. — (Under the microscope)
Includes index.
ISBN 978-1-4339-8347-4 (pbk.)
ISBN 978-1-4339-8348-1 (6-pack)
ISBN 978-1-4339-8346-7 (library binding)
1. Minerals—Juvenile literature. I. Title. II. Series: Under the microscope.
QE365.2.G53 2014
549—dc23

                                    2012047154

First Edition

Published in 2014 by
Gareth Stevens Publishing
111 East 14th Street, Suite 349
New York, NY 10003

Copyright © 2014 Gareth Stevens Publishing

Designer: Katelyn E. Reynolds
Editor: Therese Shea

Photo credits: Cover, p. 1 Michael W. Davidson/Photo Researchers/Getty Images; cover, pp. 1, 3–31 (logo) iStockphoto/Thinkstock.com; cover, pp. 1–31 (mineral image icons) Comstock/Thinkstock.com; cover, pp. 1–31 (mineral image icon) Zoonar/Thinkstock.com; cover, pp. 1–31 (mineral image icon) Spike Walker/Riser/ Getty Images; cover, pp. 1–32 (background texture) Hemera/Thinkstock.com; p. 4 Dorling Kindersley RF/Thinkstock.com; pp. 5, 7 (table) Hemera/Thinkstock. com; pp. 7 (molecule), 13, 17 (main), 27 iStockphoto/Thinkstock.com; p. 8 Brian & Mavis Bousfield/SSPL/Getty Images; p. 9 Edward Kinsman/Photo Researchers/ Getty Images; p. 11 PHGCOM/Wikipedia.com; p. 12 Thomas Northcut/Photodisc/ Thinkstock.com; p. 14 Comstock/Thinkstock.com; p. 15 Phil Degginger/Stone/ Getty Images; p. 17 (inset) G. Wanner/ScienceFoto/Getty Images; p. 18 AptTone/ Shutterstock.com; p. 19 Scimat Scimat/Photo Researchers/Getty Images; p. 21 (inset) Ra'ike/Wikipedia.com; p. 21 (main) John Cancalosi/Peter Arnold/Getty Images; p. 23 psamtik/Shutterstock.com; p. 25 Jupiterimages/Photos.com/Thinkstock.com; p. 29 Michael Abbey/Photo Researchers/Getty Images.

Printed in the United States of America

CPSIA compliance information: Batch #CS13GS: For further information contact Gareth Stevens, New York, New York at 1-800-542-2595.

CONTENTS

Words in the glossary appear in **bold** type
the first time they are used in the text.

BREAKDOWN

Living things go through cycles. They feed, grow, reproduce, and die. After death, they decay and break down into living, or organic, matter. Some of this matter ends up in soil or groundwater. Some might be food for other living things and become part of that life-form. These tiny organic bits combine and separate over and over.

Inorganic, or nonliving, matter, including minerals, goes through similar cycles. Hot, liquid rock inside Earth called magma breaks through the surface and cools into solid rock. Wind, water, and pressure tear that rock down. Some of those bits might make their way back under Earth's surface. Once there, heat and pressure transform them into another form of rock or melt them into magma again.

TYPES OF ROCKS

The rock cycle involves inorganic matter shifting between three kinds of rocks. The rocks made from cooled magma are called igneous rocks. Rocks are broken apart by wind, water, and ice. Bits of these collect and form sedimentary rocks. Sedimentary and igneous rocks can change into metamorphic rocks by means of heat and pressure. Each of the three kinds of rocks can turn into either of the other two under the right conditions.

When magma escapes onto Earth's surface, it's called lava.

ELEMENTARY

Whether it's organic matter such as a flower or inorganic matter such as the mineral calcium, atoms are the building blocks. But they're made up of even smaller units. At the center of every atom is a tiny bundle made up of particles called protons and neutrons. Electrons are a third type of particle that circles the center of the atom.

The number of protons, neutrons, and electrons in an atom affects its behavior. Under some conditions, atoms may form bonds with other atoms of the same kind. Some form bonds with different kinds of atoms. A molecule is two or more joined atoms. They keep combining to make matter. Matter made of just one kind of atom is called an element.

molecule of adrenaline

All the known elements are organized in a guide called the periodic table. They're arranged according to the number of protons in a single atom. The table begins with hydrogen, which has one proton per atom. Element 118, ununoctium, and the other highest elements aren't found in nature. They're created by scientists. The table also includes general properties of each element.

The Periodic Table of Elements

The first periodic table was presented by Russian scientist Dmitry Mendeleyev in 1869.

Period	Group 1	2	3	4	5	6	7	8	9	10	11	12	13	14	15	16	17	18
1	1 H 1.008																	2 He 4.003
2	3 Li 6.941	4 Be 9.012											5 B 10.81	6 C 12.01	7 N 14.01	8 O 16	9 F 19	10 Ne 20.18
3	11 Na 22.99	12 Mg 24.31											13 Al 26.98	14 Si 28.09	15 P 30.97	16 S 32.07	17 Cl 35.45	18 Ar 39.95
4	19 K 39.10	20 Ca 40.08	21 Sc 44.96	22 Ti 47.88	23 V 50.94	24 Cr 52	25 Mn 54.94	26 Fe 55.85	27 Co 58.47	28 Ni 58.69	29 Cu 63.55	30 Zn 65.39	31 Ga 69.72	32 Ge 72.59	33 As 74.92	34 Se 78.96	35 Br 79.9	36 Kr 83.8
5	37 Rb 85.47	38 Sr 87.62	39 Y 88.91	40 Zr 91.22	41 Nb 92.91	42 Mo 95.94	43 Tc (98)	44 Ru 101.1	45 Rh 102.9	46 Pd 106.4	47 Ag 107.9	48 Cd 112.4	49 In 114.8	50 Sn 118.7	51 Sb 121.8	52 Te 127.6	53 I 126.9	54 Xe 131.3
6	55 Cs 132.9	56 Ba 137.3	57 La 138.9	72 Hf 178.5	73 Ta 180.9	74 W 183.9	75 Re 186.2	76 Os 190.2	77 Ir 192.2	78 Pt 195.1	79 Au 197	80 Hg 200.5	81 Tl 204.4	82 Pb 207.2	83 Bi 209	84 Po (210)	85 At (210)	86 Rn (222)
7	87 Fr (223)	88 Ra (226)	89 Ac (227)	104 Rf (257)	105 Db (260)	106 Sg (263)	107 Bh (262)	108 Hs (265)	109 Mt (266)	110 Ds (271)	111 Rg (272)	112 Uub (285)	113 Uut (284)	114 Uuq (289)	115 Uup (288)	116 Uuh (292)	117 Uus 0	118 Uuo 0

Legend:
- Nonmetals
- Alkali metals
- Alkaline Earth metals
- Transition elements
- Other metals
- Metalloids
- Halogenes
- Noble gases
- Lanthanides
- Actinides

6	58 Ce 140.1	59 Pr 140.9	60 Nd 144.2	61 Pm (147)	62 Sm 150.4	63 Eu 152	64 Gd 157.3	65 Tb 158.9	66 Dy 162.5	67 Ho 164.9	68 Er 167.3	69 Tm 168.9	70 Yb 173	71 Lu 175	
7	90 Th 232	91 Pa (231)	92 U (238)	93 Np (237)	94 Pu (242)	95 Am (243)	96 Cm (247)	97 Bk (247)	98 Cf (249)	99 Es (254)	100 Fm (253)	101 Md (256)	102 No (254)	103 Lr (257)	

CARBON
BASED

Carbon is one of the most common elements on Earth. The sugars, fats, proteins, and other matter that keep people alive have carbon, and so do people's bodies. Therefore, we're called "carbon based" life-forms. People and animals even breathe out carbon in the form of carbon dioxide. Carbon can be found in several mineral forms. When carbon reshapes under great pressure, it forms diamonds.

This is a magnification of a compound called sodium silicate.

As elements come into contact with other elements, they may form bonds. Sometimes this process happens naturally. Other times, scientists join elements in labs. Everything on Earth—from orange juice to automobiles—is made from materials formed from elements. Even the same element can take many different forms. For example, both oranges and cars have iron in them!

No matter what form organic matter takes, it will always have the element carbon in it. Inorganic matter might have carbon, too, but it's not essential. Elements such as sulfur may take carbon's place in inorganic matter, as it does in some rocks. Minerals are inorganic, naturally occurring solids. A mineral is either made up of a single element or a compound, which is a mixture of elements.

DID YOU KNOW?

Scientific names for minerals are based on the mineral's core elements. Sulfates are minerals containing sulfur compounds. Minerals formed from silicon are usually called silicates.

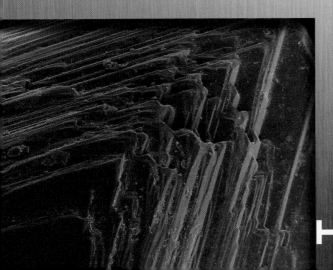

microscopic image of a diamond

MINERAL DEPOSITS

DID YOU KNOW?

A volcanic eruption can spread the mineral element sulfur across several miles of land.

Earth's surface changes constantly. Sections of its crust grind and crunch against each other, exposing some layers and burying others. These forces create cracks in the rock. In many cases, mineral-rich magma fills the cracks. The cooling magma leaves minerals mixed in with the surrounding rock.

The filled cracks are called veins. They line the rock with high concentrations of mineral, called ore. Mining operations take ore from veins in rock and **refine** the minerals. Some minerals are valuable on their own, and others can be made into useful things.

Minerals in rock can also be **dissolved** in water and easily carried away. When the water **evaporates**, the minerals form again. This kind of deposit is the main source of the world's salts.

SALT MINING

Modern mining makes table salt common today, but salt was a rare mineral for thousands of years. Mining for salt was so dangerous that many civilizations used slaves or prisoners as miners. The great value of salt created figures of speech we still use today. A great person is "worth their salt." Even the word "salary" comes from times when people were paid with salt.

By understanding what conditions form veins of ore, geologists and miners can guess where valuable ore might be found.

PROPERTIES OF MINERALS

DID YOU KNOW?

Cubic zirconia, an artificial substance with mineral properties, is an inexpensive substitute for diamonds. Nearly as hard as diamonds, it's used to make tips for special drills.

For a substance to be considered a mineral, it must meet certain requirements:

- It must be inorganic. A mineral isn't alive.

- It must form naturally. Scientists create **artificial** substances with the properties of minerals, but these aren't minerals. They're usually called synthetic.

- It must be a solid under natural conditions, not a liquid or gas. Liquid magma isn't a mineral. As it cools, substances within it become fixed, leaving behind minerals.

- It must be crystalline. That is, the atoms within it are arranged in a pattern. This gives each mineral its **unique** set of physical properties.

cubic zirconia

WHEN IS WATER A MINERAL?

Water is a liquid, not a solid, so it doesn't meet the requirements of a mineral. However, frozen water—ice—sometimes does. Naturally forming icebergs meet all the mineral requirements. So do snowflakes and frozen lakes in winter. Ice cubes from the refrigerator aren't minerals because people created them in artificial conditions. *Mineral water* is a term used for water that has dissolved minerals in it as well as some nonmineral substances.

Containing properties of both liquids and solids, mercury is a unique exception to the rule of solid minerals.

METALS

Some minerals are formed from only one element. Most single-element minerals exist as metals, such as copper, silver, gold, and platinum. Large formations of pure metal are rare in nature and usually must be refined from ore. Although solid, metals can be shaped and bent into useful and decorative forms, such as jewelry or computer circuits.

Metallurgists are people who work with metals. Metallurgists often combine pure elemental metals into metal mixes called alloys to better suit some purposes. Brass and steel are good examples of metal alloys. Gold alloys are often used in jewelry because pure gold is soft and easily broken. Silver, copper, and zinc are common ingredients in alloys.

RARE
METALS

Many people think gold is the most valuable metal on Earth. Its rarity and beauty makes it worth more than $1,000 an ounce. Yet platinum, also used in jewelry, is rarer. So is palladium, which is used in tiny amounts in cell phones. Iridium is also valuable—and often found in **meteorites**! Above them all is rhodium, a shiny metal several times more valuable than gold.

Metals are excellent conductors of heat and electricity, making them useful in electronic devices.

CRYSTAL STRUCTURE

DID YOU KNOW?

Large, slow-formed gemstones are very rare. That's why common minerals polished into gemstones like rubies and emeralds can be very valuable.

Telling one mineral from another may require a number of tests. One identifying factor is the shape of the crystals in a mineral. As atoms bond to form minerals, the arrangement of those atoms makes a specific crystal shape. The size of the crystals depends on how quickly they formed. When magma cools quickly, the crystals that form might only be visible with a microscope. If it cools slowly, the linked crystals are large. No matter their size, the crystals' shape mirrors the arrangement of the mineral's atoms.

The number of sides, or faces, of a mineral helps scientists identify the mineral, too. The **symmetry** or lack of symmetry plays a part as well. For instance, symmetrical crystals might be cubic, tetragonal, or hexagonal.

CLEAVAGE AND FRACTURE

"Cleavage" and "fracture" are terms used to describe how a mineral splits or breaks. They both reveal information about the structure of a mineral. Cleavage is the way a mineral naturally splits. Cleavage can be poor, fair, good, perfect, or eminent. Fracture describes how the edge of the break looks. Is it smooth, jagged, or crumbly? Professional jewelers use knowledge of cleavage and fracture to make beautiful shapes out of gems.

This photo shows the crystal structure of the mineral corundum.

HARD ROCK

DID YOU KNOW?

Another way to identify minerals is by their specific gravity. This compares a mineral's **density** to the density of water.

Another helpful way to identify a mineral is by its hardness. A mineral is measured by its resistance to being scratched by other substances. The Mohs' Hardness Scale ranks minerals from 1 to 10. Higher-numbered substances scratch lower-numbered substances.

The softest mineral, talc, is at the bottom of the scale. Talc breaks and scratches easily. It's often used in powders, such as talcum powder. Minerals with a hardness of 6 or more easily scratch glass. The hardest substance is diamond. Drills with diamond tips can cut through almost anything. While the scale was designed to measure mineral hardness, other objects such as pennies, nails, fingernails, and knives have a hardness rating as well.

diamond

FRIEDRICH MOHS

German geologist Friedrich Mohs created the hardness scale. In 1801, Mohs moved to Austria and took a job with a banker there. This banker had a collection of minerals he wanted organized. Mohs sorted them according to which minerals could scratch other minerals. He picked ten common minerals to represent the scale. The numbers show a mineral's hardness in relation to other minerals.

rating	mineral	other objects
1	talc	baby powder
2	gypsum	fingernail
3	calcite	copper penny
4	fluorite	iron nail
5	apatite	glass
6	orthoclase	steel file
7	quartz	steel knife
8	topaz	sandpaper
9	corundum	ruby
10	diamond	diamond jewels

This photo is a close-up of talcum powder. You can see how fragile the bits of matter look.

COLOR AND LUSTER

DID YOU KNOW?

In addition to color, luster, and streak, mineralogists might also burn a mineral's powder. The color of the flame is another clue to a mineral's identity.

Using just color to identify a mineral is misleading. Some minerals can be several different colors. Quartz can be clear, but **impurities** turn it colors such as green, blue, or pink. Since the exposed surface of some minerals changes color, minerals must be cut open in order to see their true color.

Some minerals look dull in normal light but become colorful in **ultraviolet** light. These minerals are said to be luminescent. Some minerals change colors when heated or struck.

The way in which a mineral reflects, bends, or absorbs light is known as a mineral's luster. Luster is often a better help in identifying a mineral than color is. A mineral's luster might be glassy, oily, or metallic.

STREAKING

In some cases, a mineral ground into powder is a different color than it appears in rock form. Mineralogists can use a streak plate to see that color. A streak plate is usually made of **porcelain** that hasn't been **glazed**. Scraping a mineral across a streak plate leaves a line of ground mineral for observation. Streak is another important part of mineral identification.

Fluorite and calcite glow under ultraviolet light in a mine.

MINERALS ON EARTH

DID YOU KNOW?

Although there are over 4,500 known minerals, the majority of rocks on Earth are formed from a small number of common minerals.

The most common mineral on Earth is feldspar. It's a somewhat rectangular mineral that forms from cooling magma. The type of feldspar that forms depends on which elements bond with the elements silicon and oxygen during cooling. Over half of all the minerals on Earth are some form of feldspar!

Quartz, another common mineral, is a popular find for mineral hunters. This hard mineral forms six-sided crystals and can be many different colors. Slow-forming quartz can create some very large crystals.

Because of its strong elemental bonds, mica is very heat resistant and can be used as **insulation**. Its bonds run along a plane, so sheets, or "books," of mica are made up of many thin layers.

TINY DISCOVERIES

Scientists continue to discover new minerals all the time. Some minerals form under unusual conditions and appear as tiny crystals hidden among more common minerals. You can understand why they'd be hard to find! Other minerals can't form on this planet at all. Using an electron microscope, scientists in 2011 found a mineral made only of sulfur and titanium. It came from a meteorite that crashed in Antarctica in 1969.

Quartz is a common mineral that comes in many different colors, making it a good start for a beginning rock collector.

TRICKY MINERALS

DID YOU KNOW?

Pearls aren't minerals, but they're made with the mineral aragonite. Clams and oysters coat particles trapped in their shells with aragonite.

Some kinds of minerals have unusual properties. Magnetite is a mineral formed from the elements iron and oxygen. People used a type of magnetite, called lodestone, in early compasses because it's a natural magnet. Sometimes exposure to new elements can cause changes in a mineral—it might even replace one element with another! The result is a different mineral with the shape of the first mineral. A mineral that resembles the form of a different mineral is called a pseudomorph. The Greek word *pseudes* means "false," and *morphe* means "shape."

If a mineral forms from an element that's **radioactive**, the mineral can be radioactive, too. For instance, ore containing uranium can be dangerous. However, radioactive uranium ore has important medical and military uses.

LIVING TO
NONLIVING

Though minerals are inorganic, some organic processes create substances with mineral-like properties. Under the right preserving conditions, organic tissues convert into a mineral formation, leaving a type of fossil. Petrified wood is actually organic tree matter that has turned to stone! Water carries dissolved minerals through the wood. When the water evaporates, the minerals are left behind. As the process continues, organic becomes inorganic!

Fossilized matter gives people today a look at life that existed millions of years ago. In the United States, the most famous petrified forest is located in northern Arizona.

INORGANIC
HELPING ORGANIC

Inorganic matter is very different from living, organic matter. However, plants and animals cannot live without minerals. Plants need certain substances, called nutrients, in order to grow and stay healthy. Many of these nutrients are minerals found in or added to the soil where plants grow. The minerals dissolve in groundwater and are absorbed by plants' roots. People may add fertilizer to soil if enough nutrients aren't present.

People and animals need minerals to build up their bodies much like plants do. When people and animals eat plants, their bodies take in the minerals inside the plants. Meat eaters can also get these minerals by eating animals that eat plants. To see what minerals do for your body, read the chart on page 28.

26

MINERALS AND
VITAMINS

Many people confuse minerals with vitamins, but they aren't the same. Our bodies need all vitamins, whereas only some minerals are essential. The key difference between vitamins and minerals is that people can't make their own minerals. They must get them from food. People and animals can produce many vitamins in their own bodies. For instance, simply getting enough sunlight helps people make their own vitamin D. Among other roles, minerals help the body use vitamins.

People don't need a large amount of minerals in their diet each day, but that doesn't mean minerals aren't important to keeping the body functioning well.

MINERALS
FOR THE HUMAN BODY

Mineral	How Much Daily (for ages 9–13)	Common Sources	What It Does
calcium	1,300 milligrams	dairy products, kale, Chinese cabbage, salmon	builds bones, muscles, and teeth; helps nerves and blood vessels function
chromium	25 micrograms	broccoli, potatoes, garlic	helps body use and store energy
iodine	120 micrograms	iodized salt, fish, breads, dairy	aids in development and function of brain
iron	8 milligrams	meat, beans, spinach	helps blood carry oxygen
magnesium	240 milligrams	beans, nuts, grains, green vegetables	used in over 300 body functions, including muscle and nerve function
selenium	40 micrograms	Brazil nuts, tuna, eggs	helps fight heart disease and cancer
sodium	2,300 milligrams	table salt, dairy products, vegetables	maintains nerves, muscles, and keeps water in the body
zinc	8 milligrams	seafood, beans, nuts	used to fight illness and heal wounds; aids senses of taste and smell

A milligram is one-thousandth of a gram.
A microgram is one-millionth of a gram.

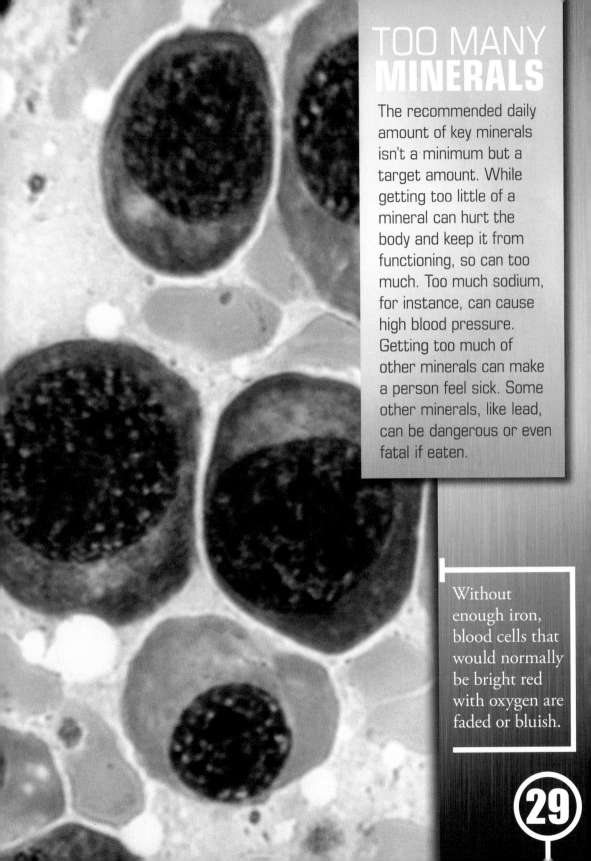

TOO MANY MINERALS

The recommended daily amount of key minerals isn't a minimum but a target amount. While getting too little of a mineral can hurt the body and keep it from functioning, so can too much. Too much sodium, for instance, can cause high blood pressure. Getting too much of other minerals can make a person feel sick. Some other minerals, like lead, can be dangerous or even fatal if eaten.

Without enough iron, blood cells that would normally be bright red with oxygen are faded or bluish.

GLOSSARY

artificial: made by people and not by nature

density: the amount of matter in a given area

dissolve: to become absorbed in a liquid

evaporate: to change from a liquid to a gas

glaze: a shiny, smooth, clear or colored coating on an object

impurity: something unwanted that is mixed in with a substance

insulation: a material that surrounds something to prevent heat, electricity, or sound from passing through

meteorite: a space rock that has reached Earth's surface

porcelain: a material used for making cups, plates, and other items

radioactive: putting out harmful energy in the form of tiny particles

refine: to produce a purer form of something by removing unwanted substances

symmetry: the property of having an equal balance of something on both sides of a dividing line or around a center

ultraviolet: a range of wavelengths in light beyond the violet end of the visible color sequence

unique: one of a kind

FOR MORE INFORMATION

BOOKS

Brown, Cynthia Light, and Nick Brown. *Explore Rocks and Minerals!* White River Junction, VT: Nomad Press, 2010.

Green, Dan. *Rocks and Minerals.* New York, NY: Kingfisher, 2009.

Tomecek, Steve. *Everything Rocks and Minerals.* Washington, DC: National Geographic, 2010.

WEBSITES

The Fascinating World of Minerals
www.mineralogicalassociation.ca/devYoung/
Learn how to get started as a rock and mineral collector, and find out how to grow your own crystals.

Mineralogy 4 Kids
www.mineralogy4kids.org
Read more about how minerals are used, and play games about minerals, too.

INDEX